KRISHNA MOHAN AVANCHA

My Story
Turning Disengaged Employees into Brand Advocates

Copyright © 2024 by Krishna Mohan Avancha

All rights reserved. No part of this publication may be reproduced, stored or transmitted in any form or by any means, electronic, mechanical, photocopying, recording, scanning, or otherwise without written permission from the publisher. It is illegal to copy this book, post it to a website, or distribute it by any other means without permission.

First edition

*This book was professionally typeset on Reedsy.
Find out more at reedsy.com*

Contents

I The Vision Trap

1 The Invisible Vision: When No One Sees Your Dream but You ... 3
2 Lost in Translation: Why Your Vision Isn't Resonating ... 8
3 The Power of "My Story" – More Than Just a CEO Bio ... 14
4 The 'Founder's Curse': How Familiarity Breeds Disconnect ... 19
5 Why Your Colleagues Aren't Buying What You're Selling ... 25

II Disconnect in the Ranks

6 Storytelling vs. Storytelling: The Tale Entrepreneurs Miss ... 33
7 The Emotional Deficit in Business Vision ... 39
8 Green Pastures Syndrome: Losing Your Best to... ... 45
9 Why Your Employees Walk Away When You Lose Your Cool ... 51

10 Relatability: The Secret Weapon of Every Great Leader — 57

III The Cost of a Weak Narrative

11 The Silent Exodus: How Misalignment Leads to Attrition — 65
12 The Mirror Effect: Seeing Your Company Through Your... — 70
13 When Passion Isn't Enough: What's Missing from Your Vision — 75
14 Vision Fatigue: Why Your Team is Checked Out — 79
15 Why Good Employees Don't Stick Around for Bad Stories — 85

IV Crafting a Relatable Vision

16 Your Story Matters: How to Make It Matter to Others — 93
17 The Leadership Vacuum: Filling It with a Compelling... — 98
18 Narrative Identity: Why Your Employees Should See Themselves... — 105
19 The Brand Advocate Formula: Turning Skeptics into Believers — 110
20 Beyond the Pitch: How to Sell the Future to Your Team — 116

I

The Vision Trap

When Your Vision Isn't Enough

One

The Invisible Vision: When No One Sees Your Dream but You

Year One: The Spark That No One Saw

It was a rainy Monday morning when I first felt the spark. That quiet whisper in my head that said, "You're destined for more." I was stuck in the same routine like everyone else—meetings, deadlines, client calls. But that day, something felt different. There was a restlessness in my gut, a knowing that I wasn't meant to be confined to this corporate cubicle. I had a vision, a dream so clear it was almost as if I could reach out and touch it. My future company, my legacy, was forming in my mind like a perfectly designed blueprint.

But there was a problem.

No one else saw it.

My Story

I remember sitting across from my best friend at lunch that same day, explaining my idea with passion. I laid it all out—the concept, the potential, the game-changing innovation. He smiled politely, nodded a few times, and said, "That sounds cool, man." But the look in his eyes told me everything I needed to know. He didn't get it. Not really. He didn't see the fire I saw.

How could he not see it? I thought. It was so vivid in my mind! It was right there.

Over the next few weeks, I pitched my vision to colleagues, mentors, family members—anyone who would listen. They smiled. They said encouraging things like, "Good luck with that" or "Sounds interesting." But deep down, I knew they didn't believe it. Worse, they didn't feel it.

This was my first lesson as an entrepreneur: just because you see the vision doesn't mean others will.

The Fog Between You and Them

The journey to realizing your vision is often a lonely one. At the start, it feels like standing in a thick fog. You see what's ahead—bright, clear, and full of promise—but everyone around you is squinting, struggling to even make out a shadow. It's frustrating. I felt like I was shouting from the top of a mountain, but no one could hear me.

This is the invisible phase of your dream. The point where your vision exists, but only in your mind. It's pristine in your head, like a puzzle with every piece perfectly aligned. But to others,

The Invisible Vision: When No One Sees Your Dream but You

it's just a box of scattered pieces that make no sense.

As the weeks rolled by, I started questioning myself. Was I wrong? Was my vision flawed? My confidence took a hit. You see, as an entrepreneur, it's natural to expect validation from those around you. You believe if you explain it well enough, show enough enthusiasm, they'll get it. They'll see it, too. But they don't.

Here's the thing: most people aren't wired to see the invisible. They're not going to believe in something that isn't real yet. They need something tangible, something they can touch and measure. And in the beginning, all you have is a feeling.

Why Others Don't See Your Vision

I started digging into the why. Why couldn't they see what I saw? Was I explaining it wrong? Was my passion coming across as overzealous? Then it hit me: the problem wasn't my vision, the problem was how I was sharing it.

I was too focused on what I was building and not why it mattered.

I was talking about the mechanics—the features, the market opportunity, the logistics—when what I should have been talking about was the heart of it. The why behind my dream.

People don't connect with ideas; they connect with purpose.

It wasn't until I reframed my vision—explaining how it was

going to change lives, why it would make a difference in the world—that I noticed a shift. Slowly, people began to listen differently. Their eyes lit up, their heads tilted in that way that signals intrigue. They still didn't fully see it, but they started to feel something.

And that was enough for the moment.

The Power of Belief in Isolation

In those early days, I learned another hard truth: you have to be okay with no one seeing the dream but you. Your vision is invisible to others not because it's not real, but because it hasn't manifested yet. They can't believe in something they can't see, and they're not supposed to.

You, however, are different. You have to believe when no one else does. You have to push forward when others shake their heads and offer polite smiles. The journey starts with you, and for a long time, it may just be you. That's okay.

Because here's the secret: visionaries don't wait for others to believe—they make it so undeniable that eventually, others have no choice but to see it.

Over time, your vision will evolve. What begins as an abstract idea in your mind will take shape. You'll refine it, adapt it, and slowly, piece by piece, the fog will start to lift. But in this first chapter, this year of invisibility, your greatest asset is your belief in yourself.

The Invisible Vision: When No One Sees Your Dream but You

Your First Job: Convince Yourself

This first year is about one thing: convincing yourself that the vision you have is worth the risk, the sacrifice, and the loneliness. It's about becoming comfortable in the space between where you are and where you want to be. When you learn to trust yourself and your vision, even when no one else does, you'll find a strength that's unshakable.

Because, let's face it—if you don't believe in your own vision with every fiber of your being, why should anyone else?

So here I am, at the end of year one, still standing in that fog. But now, the spark is a flame. The blueprint in my head is becoming clearer, and even though I'm the only one who sees it fully, I know, in time, others will.

But for now, I've got a job to do: I need to make this vision real.

Takeaway: The first step to bringing your vision to life is believing in it when no one else does. In the early stages, your dream will be invisible to others, and that's perfectly normal. Your focus should be on nurturing that spark until it becomes too bright for anyone to ignore.

Two

Lost in Translation: Why Your Vision Isn't Resonating

Year Two – The First Signs of Disconnect

It was just the second year of my entrepreneurial journey, and things were finally starting to move. I had the vision. The grand vision. It was going to change the market, disrupt the industry, and revolutionize how things were done. At least, that's what I kept telling myself. But something was off. No matter how passionately I spoke, no matter how many times I laid out the vision to my team, their faces often reflected a fog of confusion, not inspiration.

They didn't get it. Or worse—they didn't care.

I remember one afternoon, after yet another meeting where I tried to rally the team, my co-founder pulled me aside. "You

Lost in Translation: Why Your Vision Isn't Resonating

do realize nobody knows what the hell you're talking about, right?" he said. It wasn't rude, but it stung. I had spent hours crafting this vision. I could see it so clearly in my head. Why couldn't they?

That's when it hit me—my vision wasn't resonating. It wasn't sticking. And it wasn't their fault. It was mine.

The 'Lost in Translation' Problem

Looking back, I realize this was the first real test of leadership. Every entrepreneur starts with a dream, a vision, something larger than life that they're aiming for. But what happens when your team doesn't buy into that dream? What if they don't even understand it?

The disconnect wasn't because my team lacked intelligence, motivation, or talent. The disconnect was because I hadn't translated my vision into something they could latch onto, relate to, and most importantly, feel.

The problem was simple: I was speaking in my language, not theirs. I was trapped in my own head, too close to the dream to see it from their perspective. I hadn't taken the time to craft a story they could actually engage with.

This was when I realized something crucial: having a vision is one thing, but being able to communicate it in a way that resonates with others is a whole different skillset.

Speaking a Different Language

As a founder, your vision is your baby. You live and breathe

My Story

it. You think about it every hour of every day. But here's the catch: your team doesn't. They have their own lives, concerns, and day-to-day tasks to worry about. They don't eat, sleep, and dream your vision. That's why it's on you to translate it into a language they care about.

I was throwing around terms like "industry disruption" and "market transformation" like candy, thinking everyone would be just as excited as I was. But what I missed was that my team was drowning in the details. My abstract vision didn't connect with their realities—how did this vision translate into their daily work? What did it mean for their roles? How did it impact them personally?

And let's be honest—without those connections, no one's going to care.
   The Emotional Disconnect

More than anything, the problem was emotional. I was so focused on the what that I forgot the why. I knew why I was passionate about the vision—because it was my vision. But my team? They weren't emotionally invested because I hadn't shared my own excitement in a way that could make them feel like part of the journey.

Imagine sitting in a meeting where someone talks for an hour about an abstract dream that doesn't directly relate to your day-to-day challenges. You'd zone out too, right?

I remember a specific moment when I realized this emotional gap. I had spent nearly half an hour explaining the long-term

Lost in Translation: Why Your Vision Isn't Resonating

vision during a weekly meeting. I was so pumped up, I expected a round of applause. Instead, I got blank stares and a few awkward nods. My CTO finally spoke up: "Okay, but what are we supposed to do now?"

It hit me hard. I had been selling them the future, but not the path to get there. They couldn't see themselves in my dream because I hadn't connected the dots.

How I Started to Fix It

The first step to fixing a broken vision? Listen.

I started holding one-on-one sessions with key team members to get their perspective. I wasn't asking for feedback on the vision itself—that would've been too abstract. Instead, I asked them what their concerns were, what they were struggling with, and how they viewed the company's direction. Their responses were eye-opening.

Most of them believed in the company, but they couldn't connect with the grand vision I was preaching. It felt too far away, too lofty. They needed to understand how their work played a role in getting there. Without that connection, my words were just noise.

Translating the Vision

Here's what I learned: To get your vision to resonate, you have to translate it into practical, personal, and actionable terms. Here's how I started doing that:

Clarify the Story: I rewrote my vision in simpler terms,

stripping away the jargon and focusing on the why behind the company's mission. Why were we doing what we were doing? What problem were we solving? I needed my team to not just understand this but feel it.

Tie it to the Present: I started mapping the vision to the present. Instead of talking about "industry disruption," I spoke about what our work today meant for our success tomorrow. I shared stories of companies that had gone through the same journey—tying their struggles to our current situation, so my team could see the parallels.

Connect It to Personal Goals: I started asking my team what they wanted to achieve. Did they want to learn new skills? Did they want to grow their careers? I connected these personal goals to the larger vision. The dream became not just mine but theirs, because they could now see how it benefited them personally.

Regular Check-ins: Vision isn't a one-time speech. I started making sure the vision was part of regular conversations—not just grand meetings. It became woven into the fabric of everything we did, so it wasn't some abstract idea but something real and present.

Lessons Learned

By the end of the second year, I realized that vision alone doesn't inspire. It's the story behind the vision, the people involved in the journey, and the emotional investment that creates true connection.

Lost in Translation: Why Your Vision Isn't Resonating

If your vision isn't resonating, it's not because your employees don't believe in you. It's because you haven't shown them a story they can believe in.

As an entrepreneur, I thought my job was to tell the vision. What I learned was that my real job was to translate it.

End of Year Two – The Journey Continues

Three

The Power of "My Story" — More Than Just a CEO Bio

It's not what you tell people; it's what they hear that makes the difference."

Every entrepreneur has a story. You've likely told yours hundreds of times—how you built your company from the ground up, struggled through sleepless nights, and chased down investors when everyone else gave up. But if that's all your story is—a highlight reel of your triumphs—then you're missing the real power behind it. Your story isn't just about you—it's about what it means to others.

Let me take you back to a time when I thought my story was bulletproof.

The Birth of My Vision

The Power of "My Story" — More Than Just a CEO Bio

When I started my company, my bio was everything. It was my armor, my proof of success, and the reason people should trust me. I believed that if my employees knew how much I had overcome to get where I was, they would be inspired. I had every detail perfectly lined up in my "about" section: the garage startup, the sacrifices, the first big client. Every time someone asked, I would recount these moments with pride, as if they alone could build loyalty.

And yet, something wasn't right.

Despite my team nodding in agreement and congratulating me on my journey, there was always a subtle disconnect. It showed in their lack of engagement, their quiet quitting, and their slow but steady drift toward the door. I was frustrated. After all, hadn't I shared my story with them? Wasn't that supposed to inspire them to stay?

Beyond the Bio: The Missing Connection

Then, one day, while having coffee with a former employee who had left for what he called "greener pastures," I got the gut punch I wasn't expecting. "Your story is great," he said, "but it never felt like ours." He wasn't being harsh—just honest. My story was my story. It wasn't the team's. It didn't resonate with the struggles they were facing or the vision they wanted to be part of. My story was about survival and victory, but it wasn't relatable.

I realized that to most of them, my CEO bio felt like a distant achievement, not something they could see themselves in. My story had all the heroic elements but lacked one critical component: emotional connection. What was missing was the part where they could see themselves in the narrative—not as spectators but as participants.

Rewriting the Narrative: Shifting the Spotlight

I knew something had to change. It wasn't enough for me to be the hero of the story anymore. I needed to make my employees co-heroes, so they didn't just witness the journey—they lived it.

Instead of telling them about my sleepless nights, I started asking them about theirs. Instead of sharing my big client wins, I asked them to share their own challenges. My "story" became a dialogue, not a monologue. We began to weave together a narrative where their successes, struggles, and aspirations were part of the fabric that made the company thrive. It was less about me and more about us.

I also learned the value of vulnerability. For so long, I thought my story had to be all about strength and perseverance. But as soon as I started sharing the tough moments—the times I felt like quitting, the times I made the wrong call—that's when the real magic happened. My employees began to open up, too. They felt safer sharing their own fears, mistakes, and triumphs. That's when I knew that my story had shifted from a CEO bio to something much more powerful: a shared narrative that everyone could relate to.

Storytelling as a Leadership Tool

I learned that being a great storyteller isn't just about being a great speaker or having an epic tale to tell. It's about being able to connect the dots between your story and the lives of those who work alongside you. When your team feels like they are a part of your journey—and that your journey is a part of theirs—everything changes. Engagement skyrockets. People become more committed because they feel they are contributing to something bigger than themselves.

Storytelling in leadership isn't about crafting the perfect narrative to impress investors or media outlets. It's about creating a living story that evolves with your team. It's about making sure that the vision isn't just something you see, but something they can see themselves building with you.

The Ripple Effect

After this shift, I noticed a ripple effect throughout the company. My story was no longer about me, and the team knew it. I didn't have to push for them to invest emotionally anymore—they were already in it. Employees started taking more ownership of their roles. They were no longer just executing tasks; they were adding layers to the story, bringing their own creativity and solutions to the table.

Brand advocacy grew organically. My team began sharing our story with others—friends, family, potential hires—without any prompting. They believed in the vision because they felt part of it, not just like bystanders watching a movie from the cheap seats. They had front-row seats and even some writing credits.

How You Can Do It Too

The power of "My Story" isn't about creating the perfect CEO bio—it's about crafting a narrative that others can see themselves in. Here's how you can start:

My Story

Make Your Story a Dialogue – Invite your team to contribute to the narrative. Ask about their experiences and how they see the company's future.

Be Vulnerable – Share your struggles, not just your successes. Authenticity breeds trust.

Connect the Dots – Find ways to link your story to the everyday experiences of your employees. Make them feel like they are co-owners of the journey.

Celebrate Collective Wins – Don't just highlight your milestones. Shine a spotlight on the team's contributions and how they shaped the company.

Evolve the Story – Your story should never be static. As your company grows, so should the narrative. Let your team's achievements be a part of that evolution.

In the end, your bio might get you admiration, but a truly compelling story will win hearts. And winning hearts is how you turn employees into advocates, and advocates into lifelong believers. After all, when the story is powerful enough, people won't just want to be part of it—they'll want to write it with you.

Four

The 'Founder's Curse': How Familiarity Breeds Disconnect

I remember the early days like it was yesterday. The energy was palpable, the excitement contagious. It felt like everyone around me was feeding off my passion, as if the vision I had was sparking something profound in them. But as the months rolled on, something shifted. Meetings became quieter, the enthusiasm dulled, and worse, I began hearing rumblings about people "considering other opportunities."

The baffling part? I hadn't changed. The vision hadn't changed. If anything, I was more determined than ever. So what went wrong?

The Curse of Being 'Too Close'

Here's the irony of entrepreneurship: the more intimately you know your vision, the more likely you are to assume everyone else gets it the same way you do. That's where the 'Founder's Curse' comes in. You're so familiar with the intricacies of your business, the grand vision you crafted, that you stop explaining it in ways that resonate. You stop selling it altogether, thinking everyone's already bought in. After all, you live and breathe this stuff—so why can't they?

The disconnect is born from the very thing that fueled your success: your deep, personal relationship with the vision. It's like trying to share your favorite movie with a friend. You know every line, every plot twist, every emotional beat, but when they don't react the same way, you're left wondering if they watched the same film. Spoiler alert: they did, but they haven't spent years memorizing the script like you have.

From Visionary to Tunnel Vision

As founders, we tend to get tunnel vision. We get so wrapped up in the day-to-day grind that we assume everyone else sees the bigger picture as clearly as we do. But they don't. For them, it's a job, a role, a paycheck. Unless we continuously bring them back to the "why" of what we're doing, they lose touch with the mission, and eventually, they lose interest.

I didn't realize it then, but over time, my team stopped being inspired. They stopped feeling connected to the company's purpose. Sure, I was still fired up about where we were headed, but I had stopped sharing that fire. I assumed they still felt it.

That's when it hit me: I wasn't telling the story anymore.

The Founder's Curse: How Familiarity Breeds Disconnect

The Familiarity Trap

It's human nature to get comfortable with what you know. Think about your closest relationships—family, best friends, or even a spouse. At some point, you stop explaining the little things because you assume they already know. You stop going out of your way to show appreciation because it's implied. You stop telling them how much they mean to you because, well, they should already know, right?

Wrong.

In business, the same thing happens. I started taking for granted that my employees were still onboard with the original mission, still passionate about our goals. I forgot that they needed constant reinforcement of why they were here in the first place. The founder's curse had taken hold, and I was blind to it.

Familiarity Breeds Disconnect

As a founder, your relationship with your vision is intensely personal. For you, it's not just a business—it's your life's work, your passion project, your reason for getting up in the morning. But for your employees? It's a job. Sure, it might be a job they enjoy, but unless they feel personally invested, they'll never see it the way you do.

This is where the disconnect happens. The more familiar you become with your vision, the less you feel the need to communicate it. But what's second nature to you is still new to them. And if you don't keep nurturing that connection, it withers.

I thought that just by being in the room, my passion would be enough. That they'd feel it by osmosis. But no matter how much I lived and breathed the company, they needed to hear it, see it, and feel it for themselves—repeatedly. The closer I got to the vision, the further I drifted from my team.

Breaking the Curse

So how do you break the founder's curse? How do you stop familiarity from breeding disconnect? Here's what I learned the hard way:

Repetition is Your Friend

You may be tired of telling your story, but that's because you've lived it over and over again. Your employees, on the other hand, need to hear it fresh every time. Just because you know every chapter of the company's journey doesn't mean they do. Repetition is key. You need to keep reminding them why the company exists, where it's headed, and how they play a crucial role in it.

Create Rituals Around Your Story

Rituals aren't just for holidays. In business, creating regular moments to revisit the company's mission and vision keeps it alive. Whether it's quarterly all-hands meetings, weekly leadership briefings, or even informal check-ins, find ways to bring the story front and center again and again. These rituals anchor the team to the company's purpose and keep the vision from fading into the background.

The Founder's Curse: How Familiarity Breeds Disconnect

Tailor the Story to Your Audience

Not everyone connects with the same message in the same way. Some employees will resonate with the company's social impact, while others are driven by growth opportunities or innovation. Understand the different motivations within your team and tailor your storytelling accordingly. It's not a one-size-fits-all approach.

Make the Story About Them

You know the vision is about more than just you, but do your employees feel that? Are they co-authors of the story, or just footnotes? The more you make your vision relatable and inclusive, the more employees will feel a sense of ownership over it. Make it clear that their contributions are what will turn the dream into reality.

Keep the Passion Alive

Your team looks to you for energy. If you're not excited, they won't be either. No matter how familiar you are with the vision, you need to show up every day with the same passion and intensity you had on day one. You are the emotional anchor of the business—if you're not bringing the fire, neither will they.

Conclusion: Overcoming the Founder's Curse

I learned this lesson the hard way: familiarity can breed disinterest if you're not careful. As a founder, your proximity to the vision makes it easy to forget that others need constant reminders, constant re-engagement, and a personal connection to the story. Without that, they drift. They lose faith. They look elsewhere for something that feels more alive.

My Story

The solution? Keep telling the story. Tell it louder, tell it better, and most importantly—tell it often. Your vision needs to be more than just yours; it has to belong to everyone in the room. If you can't break the founder's curse, your vision will remain just that—a dream that no one else is invested in.

Five

Why Your Colleagues Aren't Buying What You're Selling

Year 5: The Silent Disconnect

The fifth year of my entrepreneurial journey felt like walking through a fog. Everything looked fine on the surface, but something was off. My vision, once burning bright and clear, seemed to fall flat whenever I shared it with my team. I had grown comfortable with my ideas and assumed they would too. I thought my colleagues, the ones who had been with me since the beginning, would automatically understand where I was coming from. But here we were, five years in, and I found myself frustrated. No matter how many times I pitched my vision, it wasn't sticking.

I remember one particular meeting. I had spent hours preparing a new strategy that I was sure would excite my core team—those colleagues who had been by my side since day one. I laid it all out, from the new product line to our growth projections and the branding overhaul. I could feel the energy pumping through my veins as I spoke. But when I looked around the room, their faces told a different story: nodding heads, blank expressions, and the eerie silence of forced politeness. There was no spark. No excitement. Nothing.

As I left that meeting, I couldn't shake the feeling that something was deeply wrong. Why weren't they buying into the vision I had spent years crafting? What had changed?

The Comfort of Familiarity

In the first few years, things were different. Back then, every idea felt revolutionary, every pivot exciting. My colleagues were equally passionate, feeding off my energy. But by year five, we had grown comfortable. They had seen the ups and downs, witnessed the long nights and endless pitches. And I had become so entrenched in my own story that I had forgotten they needed more than a PowerPoint presentation to stay engaged.

The problem was clear, though it took me a while to see it: I had been telling the same story for years, without considering that my colleagues' roles in that story had evolved. When we first started, we were all scrappy dreamers. But now, five years in, they had grown into experts in their own right, with their own dreams, their own challenges. The old narrative no longer fit.

The Assumption of Buy-In

Why Your Colleagues Aren't Buying What You're Selling

I had made one fatal mistake: I assumed that because they worked with me, they believed in what I believed. I thought we were on the same page simply because we had the same job titles, sat in the same meetings, and shared the same company name. But in reality, they weren't just extensions of my vision. They were people with their own stories, and I had failed to connect my vision to theirs.

At year five, something shifted. It became clear that my colleagues weren't resisting my ideas because they didn't understand them—they were resisting because they didn't feel connected to the vision anymore. I was the one who had lived with it, nurtured it, obsessed over it every single day. But for them, the vision had become just another task on their to-do list.

The Dreaded Disconnect

The disconnect happens gradually, and it's not just about the big, obvious things like company strategy. It's about the little things—the meetings where everyone zones out, the enthusiastic emails that get one-word replies, the feedback sessions where no one has much to say. Slowly, you start to realize that your vision is no longer their vision.

As I thought about it more, I realized this: they weren't rejecting my ideas—they just didn't feel included in the process anymore. I had been so focused on selling the "what" of the vision that I had forgotten about the "why." And without the "why," there's no emotional buy-in.

My Story

People don't just work for a paycheck, and they don't follow a leader just because they're told to. They follow a leader when they feel connected to something bigger, something meaningful. And that's where I had failed—I hadn't updated the story. I hadn't brought them along on the journey of why this vision still mattered, and more importantly, why it mattered to them.

The Role of Relatability

If there's one thing I've learned by year five, it's that relatability is the glue that holds everything together. You can be the smartest person in the room, the most innovative, the most visionary—but if people can't see themselves in your story, they're not going to invest in it.

I had to take a hard look at myself and ask: How am I telling the story? I realized that my narrative was all about me—my vision, my ideas, my goals. What I hadn't done was frame that vision in a way that showed how it benefited them.

I started having one-on-one conversations with my team members, really listening to their aspirations, fears, and frustrations. What did they want from this journey? Where did they see themselves in five years? Once I had a clearer picture of their individual stories, I realized how easy it was to reframe my vision. It wasn't about selling my dream; it was about weaving their dreams into the larger tapestry.

Building Bridges, Not Walls

From that point forward, I began crafting my pitches differently.

Why Your Colleagues Aren't Buying What You're Selling

Instead of standing at the front of the room, declaring my vision like some grand proclamation, I started leading with questions: What does success look like to you? How do you see this idea fitting into your role? What excites you about this direction? The more I listened, the more I was able to see the gaps in my narrative and adjust it to meet their needs.

It wasn't about diluting the vision—it was about building bridges between my story and theirs. When I did that, everything changed. Suddenly, the blank stares turned into excited discussions. The polite nods became real engagement. My team didn't just hear the vision; they started to see themselves as a part of it.

The Fifth-Year Revelation

Year five taught me the most important lesson of my entrepreneurial journey: your vision is only as strong as the story you tell, and that story is only powerful when it's shared. Not told at people, but shared with them.

By learning to tell "my story" in a way that brought my colleagues into the fold, I turned a passive audience into an active team. They weren't just buying what I was selling anymore—they were helping me sell it to the world.

II

Disconnect in the Ranks

Why Employees Walk Away

Six

Storytelling vs. Storytelling: The Tale Entrepreneurs Miss

Year 6. By now, I thought I had mastered the art of storytelling. I could rattle off my company's origin story, pitch our vision in my sleep, and dazzle investors with my grand plans for the future. Yet, despite my storytelling efforts, my employees still felt disconnected. The office buzzed with the sound of productivity, but I could sense a distance—a growing void. Something was missing, and I couldn't put my finger on it.

I thought I was telling stories, but in truth, I was missing the essence of storytelling that resonates with people on a deeper level.

The Realization

It wasn't until one of my most talented employees, let's call him Raj, handed in his resignation that the cracks in my storytelling began to show. Raj was one of those key people—the kind you know you can't afford to lose. I was confused. He had always seemed engaged, interested, and even excited about the company's future. But now, he was leaving for what he called "a more meaningful opportunity."

"More meaningful?" I thought. How could he not find meaning in what we were building here?

I sat down with Raj for an exit interview, determined to understand what had gone wrong. As we spoke, it became clear. While I had been telling the company's story, I hadn't been telling his story. I wasn't making him—or anyone else—feel like a part of the bigger picture. My storytelling was all about the company, the grand vision, and me. I had missed one of the most crucial elements of storytelling: inclusion.

The Key Element: Inclusion in Storytelling

In my mind, I had been crafting a compelling narrative. After all, I knew how to tell stories—at least I thought I did. But there's a subtle difference between telling a story and inviting others to see themselves within that story. That's what I had been missing: making the people around me feel like co-authors of the story we were creating.

The key element I discovered that year was the power of inclusion in storytelling. This was the step I had overlooked—the simple but profound act of weaving the personal experiences, aspirations, and values of my team into the company's broader narrative. Once I understood this, everything changed.

The "We" in the Story

Storytelling vs. Storytelling: The Tale Entrepreneurs Miss

Great storytelling isn't just about presenting a compelling vision; it's about making others feel like they have a stake in that vision. The moment an individual can see themselves as part of the unfolding story, they become invested in its outcome. It's no longer your dream—it's our dream.

In the same way that characters in a novel come alive because we understand their motivations, fears, and desires, employees need to feel like their stories are part of the company's DNA. It's not enough for them to just understand where the company is headed—they need to feel like they're personally involved in driving that direction.

And that was my epiphany: I hadn't made space for their stories.
Why Inclusion Helps Build Stronger Stories (and Teams)

The more I researched the power of storytelling in business, the more it became clear that inclusion wasn't just a "nice-to-have"—it was fundamental to building loyalty, fostering engagement, and driving commitment. When employees feel that their individual stories matter, they're far more likely to contribute passionately and stick around for the long haul.

The beauty of inclusive storytelling is that it naturally leads to co-ownership. When you involve your team in shaping the narrative, they become emotionally connected to the outcomes. They feel a sense of pride and responsibility for the direction of the company, because they're not just following orders—they're actively crafting the future alongside you.
A Practical Step for Inclusive Storytelling

My Story

I took this realization and turned it into a simple, actionable step that transformed my storytelling: I started hosting "Story Circles" every month. These weren't meetings to discuss KPIs or strategy (we had plenty of those). Instead, these sessions were spaces for my team to share their stories—about why they joined the company, what they hoped to achieve, and what inspired them.

I listened. I asked questions. I learned about their personal goals and found ways to connect their individual narratives to the broader company mission. And slowly but surely, I began to rewrite the story of our company—not as the story of one founder with a vision, but as a collective story that everyone could see themselves in.

Here's how Story Circles helped me include my team in the story:

Creating shared ownership: When I acknowledged their dreams, it made the company vision more personal to each employee. We weren't just building my company; we were building our legacy.

Uncovering hidden motivations: Employees often have hidden talents or desires that don't come out in day-to-day tasks. Story Circles gave them a space to share their aspirations, allowing me to align their personal goals with the company's objectives.

Building emotional connections: By listening to their stories, I was able to forge deeper emotional connections. People are loyal to those who see and value their personal journey.

Storytelling vs. Storytelling: The Tale Entrepreneurs Miss

Why This Helps Build Your Story

As an entrepreneur, you need to think of storytelling not as a monologue, but as a dialogue. The more inclusive your narrative is, the more powerful it becomes. Here's why this matters for you:

Inclusion deepens commitment: When people see themselves in the story, they become committed to its success. Your employees will no longer feel like outsiders following someone else's vision. They'll become co-creators, which leads to higher loyalty and lower turnover.

It strengthens company culture: A shared story is a powerful glue that holds your team together. When everyone feels like they're contributing to a collective mission, it fosters a stronger, more cohesive culture.

It drives innovation: When employees are part of the storytelling process, they feel empowered to contribute ideas and innovations that can drive the company forward. Their unique perspectives enrich the narrative, sparking creativity and growth.

The Tale Entrepreneurs Miss

So many entrepreneurs fall into the trap of thinking that just because they've shared their vision, they've done enough. But as I learned in Year 6, there's a vast difference between telling people what you want to achieve and showing them how their story fits into that vision.

My Story

It was only after I discovered the power of inclusion that my company's story truly began to take off. Employees who once seemed distant became deeply engaged. The company's story was no longer just a tale I was telling; it was a collective journey that we were all writing together.

The tale most entrepreneurs miss isn't that their vision isn't good enough—it's that their storytelling is incomplete. Without the inclusion of those around you, your story will remain just that—yours. But when you invite others into the narrative, it becomes something far greater: ours.

Seven

The Emotional Deficit in Business Vision

It was the seventh year of my startup journey, and I was standing in front of my small but talented team, eagerly pitching the company's vision for the next five years. The enthusiasm on my end was palpable. Every word, every slide of the PowerPoint presentation was carefully crafted, filled with numbers, projections, and lofty goals. I believed I had nailed it. After all, what's not to love about ambition and innovation?

But there was something wrong. As I scanned the room, I could see blank stares, fidgeting hands, and a few quiet sighs. They weren't connecting. It felt like I was talking to a brick wall. I had poured my heart into this vision, but there was no spark on the other side. My vision felt flat in their eyes. For the life of me, I couldn't understand why.

My Story

The Emotional Deficit

That's when I realized that while my vision had all the strategic brilliance in the world, it lacked something fundamental: emotion. I was presenting numbers, facts, and future possibilities, but there was no soul to the story. I didn't tell them why they should care. My words, though clever, didn't tug at their hearts or stir their passions.

This emotional deficit in my storytelling was driving a wedge between me and my team. When people can't emotionally connect with a story, they can't connect with the vision behind it. And when they can't connect with the vision, they lose interest in the mission. Employees may follow instructions, but they won't go above and beyond. They won't fight for the dream because it doesn't resonate with them on a human level.

In my rush to present a polished, strategic plan, I had forgotten the second key element of effective storytelling: Emotional Resonance.

Discovering the Second Key to Storytelling: Emotional Resonance

"People will forget what you said, people will forget what you did, but people will never forget how you made them feel."
— Maya Angelou

This quote, more than anything, encapsulates the second key step in storytelling. Emotional resonance isn't about how great your plan is; it's about how your story makes others feel. It's the

The Emotional Deficit in Business Vision

moment when the listener not only understands what you're saying but also feels it deeply within themselves.

Emotional resonance doesn't just make a story memorable—it makes it personal. And that is the magic that turns passive employees into emotionally invested advocates. I didn't understand this at the time, but learning how to infuse my story with emotion would be one of the greatest breakthroughs in my leadership.

Here's how I figured it out:
  Why Emotional Resonance Matters in Storytelling

Every great story—whether it's in a movie, a novel, or a business pitch—has an emotional core. It's not the plot or the characters alone that stick with people; it's the way those things make them feel. This is true in business storytelling too. When you pitch a vision, you're not just talking about the "what" and "how" of the future; you're shaping how that future feels to the people you're speaking to.

If your employees can't emotionally invest in your story, they will struggle to invest in your vision. When people feel emotionally connected, they:

Care deeply about outcomes.
  Engage with purpose.
  Contribute their creativity and energy.
  Feel like they're part of something greater than themselves.

In the early days, I was too focused on being rational and

strategic. But a business vision devoid of emotion is like a song without a melody—sure, it has lyrics, but it's not moving anyone.

How Emotional Resonance Helped Me Tell My Story

Once I realized the power of emotional resonance, I started to rethink how I approached every meeting and every conversation with my team. Instead of just sharing future projections or product goals, I began by sharing the "why" behind them.

I shared personal stories—moments when the business meant everything to me, times I stayed awake all night because I believed in what we were building. I talked about the impact our work could have on real people, not just market share. I let myself be vulnerable, expressing how much this journey mattered to me. And I did something that was very uncomfortable for me at first: I admitted that I didn't have all the answers.

Slowly, I started to see a shift. When I spoke with emotion, my team started listening differently. They were no longer just hearing the words; they were feeling the urgency, the passion, and the belief that this business wasn't just another job—it was a cause worth fighting for.

How Emotional Resonance Can Help You Build Your Story

To build emotional resonance in your story, you don't need to be a master orator. What you need is to tap into the human side of your vision. Here's how you can do it:

Get Personal: Share your personal connection to the vision.

The Emotional Deficit in Business Vision

What does it mean to you on a human level? Why do you wake up excited (or anxious) every day? People follow people, not just plans.

Talk About Impact: Instead of just talking numbers or goals, talk about the impact. How will this vision change lives, create opportunities, or solve real-world problems? Paint a picture of the future where your employees are the heroes of the story.

Vulnerability is Power: Don't be afraid to share your struggles, your uncertainties, and even your failures. Vulnerability builds trust and makes you relatable. When your team sees your humanity, they'll feel more connected to your vision.

Use Emotion in Your Language: Words matter. Instead of saying, "We need to hit a 20% growth target," say, "If we achieve this, we'll be helping thousands of families build better lives." Focus on the human side of your goals.

Create Shared Meaning: Make sure your employees see themselves in your story. Create a shared narrative where they feel like an essential part of the journey, not just a cog in the machine.

How Emotional Resonance Shifted My Team's Engagement

Once I began incorporating emotional resonance into my storytelling, the dynamic of our team shifted dramatically. Instead of merely attending meetings, my employees started contributing to them. They began taking ownership, suggesting ideas, and pushing the boundaries of what was possible. They weren't just working for the company; they were working with me, and for a shared vision that they believed in.

Emotional resonance had unlocked the missing piece in my leadership. It was no longer about how I could get my team to follow my vision, but about how I could invite them into a shared story—one where they felt emotionally invested, valued, and understood.

As I would later learn, emotional resonance wasn't just a "nice-to-have" in business; it was the bridge between disengaged employees and a passionate, loyal team. And that bridge made all the difference.

In this chapter, we learned the importance of the second key element of storytelling: Emotional Resonance. Without it, a vision feels like a hollow idea, but with it, your story becomes a powerful tool for building deeper connections with your team. This emotional buy-in transforms your employees from passive participants to passionate advocates, ultimately making your business stronger and more resilient.

Eight

Green Pastures Syndrome: Losing Your Best to Miscommunication

"I thought I had it all figured out—an exciting vision, a growing company, and the right team. But one by one, the people I trusted the most slipped away. What was I missing?"

It was the third year of my company's journey. We were on the cusp of something great—or so I thought. Growth was good, but the revolving door of talent was becoming a concern. Some of my top performers had just handed in their resignations, and each time, I was blindsided. These weren't just employees—they were my confidants, the people who had been with me from the early days, who had fought through the trenches and believed in what we were building. Or at least I thought they did.

It wasn't until a candid conversation with one of my soon-to-be former employees that the truth came out. "I just don't see where I fit in anymore," she said, with a look of genuine remorse. "I know you've got big plans, but it feels like I'm just… here. And honestly, I think I could be doing something more meaningful elsewhere."

There it was—the elephant in the room. Despite all the team meetings, strategy sessions, and passionate speeches, my people weren't seeing their place in the vision. They felt like cogs in a machine rather than co-owners of the dream.

This is what I came to call the Green Pastures Syndrome. My employees weren't leaving because they didn't like their jobs or the company—they were leaving because they couldn't connect their own personal journeys with the larger vision I was selling. Miscommunication wasn't about poor instructions or lack of clarity in tasks; it was about a failure to communicate their role in the bigger picture.

The Element That Changes Everything: Relatability

In storytelling, there are key elements that every great narrative must have, and one of them is relatability. It was the third step in the storytelling process that I learned, and it turned out to be the missing piece in my company's growth strategy. Relatability is the bridge between your vision and the people who need to carry it forward. It's not just about getting people to listen—it's about getting them to see themselves in the story you're telling.

Without this step, your story remains distant, abstract, and unattainable. You can paint the grandest vision, but if the people hearing it don't know where they fit in, they'll tune out—or worse, they'll walk away, searching for greener pastures where they feel valued, connected, and, most importantly, involved.

Why Relatability Matters in Storytelling

Relatability is the emotional glue that binds your story to your audience. In this case, my audience wasn't a room full of investors or potential clients—it was my employees. These were the people who needed to believe in the vision more than anyone else, but instead, they were slipping through my fingers because I had failed to make my story theirs.

When a story is relatable, it:

Creates Ownership: People need to feel like they have a stake in the outcome. In business, this means showing your team how their individual efforts are not just important but essential to the company's overall success. By making the story about them, you transform your vision from something they work for into something they work with.

Fosters Emotional Engagement: Relatability pulls at the heartstrings. People don't just stay because of a paycheck; they stay because they care. When they can relate to the story you're telling, they invest emotionally. They become part of something bigger, which ignites their passion and fuels their commitment.

Turns Miscommunication into Clarity: Miscommunication is not always about a lack of information. Often, it's about information that doesn't click. By focusing on relatability, you make sure that your message doesn't just make sense, but that it matters. This eliminates confusion, misunderstandings, and the feeling that their role is replaceable.

Aligns Personal and Professional Goals: Employees leave when they see a disconnect between their personal ambitions and the company's vision. But if they can relate to the journey you're taking them on, their goals align with yours, creating a shared path to success.

Bringing Relatability into Your Story

At this point in my journey, I had learned that simply sharing a vision wasn't enough. To keep my team invested, I needed to weave their personal stories into the larger company narrative. And to do that, I had to make the vision relatable to each of them.

The third step in storytelling—relatability—became my guiding principle in reshaping the company's internal narrative. Here's how I did it, and how you can, too:

Find the Common Ground: Look at your team and ask yourself: What do they care about? What are their personal goals, ambitions, and dreams? The key is to connect your company's story to these individual aspirations. I started having one-on-one conversations with my team members, learning what motivated them. It wasn't about changing the company vision; it was about finding intersections between the vision and their lives.

Make Their Role Personal: Once I understood their personal ambitions, I began reframing their roles within the company's story. I explained how their unique skills and contributions weren't just helping the company succeed, but also helping them reach their own goals. It became less about "working for me" and more about "working for themselves within the larger story."

Incorporate Their Wins into the Company's Story: Every time an employee achieved something, I made sure to highlight how it contributed to the bigger picture. When they could see their personal wins as part of the company's journey, the entire story felt more cohesive and shared. This wasn't my dream anymore—it was our dream.

Share the Future in a Way They Can Relate To: I stopped talking about the future of the company in vague, grand terms, and started being specific about how each of them would fit into that future. They didn't just want to hear about the "company's growth" or "next phase"; they wanted to know what that meant for them personally. And once I tied those together, the future became something they could actually see themselves being part of.

How Relatability Can Save Your Best People

As soon as I embraced relatability as the core element of storytelling, everything started to shift. I wasn't just shouting my vision from the rooftop, hoping it would resonate with someone. I was inviting people into the story and making it theirs.

The people who had once been looking for greener pastures?

My Story

They stayed. Not because the pay was better or the workload lighter, but because they saw a future in which they were central characters—co-authors of the company's success, and more importantly, their own.

And that, I realized, was the key to stopping the constant turnover: not just having a compelling vision, but having a relatable story that everyone could see themselves in.

"The moment I stopped making it about just my story, the story started to come alive. Now, the journey is no longer mine alone—it's ours. And that's when everything began to change."

Nine

Why Your Employees Walk Away When You Lose Your Cool

It was the ninth year in the company, and everything seemed to be moving faster than expected. The company had just landed a huge client, projects were stacking up, and deadlines were tighter than a chokehold. I was running on coffee and adrenaline, and my team was too. But something started to crack—and it wasn't just the deadlines or the workload. It was me.

One Monday morning, the latest project hit a snag. We were about to miss a deadline, and my mind raced as I tried to calculate the impact. My frustration brewed, boiling up with every update that seemed worse than the last. Finally, in the middle of a meeting, I snapped. My voice raised, words sharper than they should've been. I didn't scream, but the room grew so silent you could hear the weight of my words drop. My

My Story

frustration wasn't just directed at the work; it felt personal, and everyone could feel it.

Over the next week, I noticed something unsettling. My employees weren't just avoiding eye contact—they were mentally checking out. Emails were colder, work was less creative, and the once buzzing energy in the office felt stale. A week later, two of my best team members handed in their resignations. When I asked why they were leaving, they gave me the usual, diplomatic answers—new opportunities, greener pastures, all that jazz. But I knew the truth. They were walking away because I had lost my cool.

The Fourth Element of Storytelling: Emotional Control

What I didn't know then, but later learned as part of my journey, is that storytelling—especially as a leader—is not just about sharing your vision. It's about controlling the emotional climate in the room, especially in tough moments. This brings me to the fourth key element of storytelling: Emotional Control.

Just like a good story can take you on a journey of highs and lows without ever losing the audience, a great leader knows how to guide their team through emotional rollercoasters. The moment you let your emotions get the best of you, you lose control of the narrative. And in that moment, when your employees see their leader unravel, they lose faith—not just in you, but in the story you're telling about the company's future.

Why Emotional Control is Crucial

In storytelling, a great storyteller understands the power of emotions. They know when to pull on the heartstrings, when to create tension, and when to release it for a satisfying resolution. The same goes for leadership. Emotional control isn't about bottling up your feelings—it's about managing them effectively so they don't overwhelm the story you're trying to tell.

Here's what I learned the hard way:

Your Mood Sets the Tone: As a leader, you are the narrator of your company's story. If you're erratic or unpredictable, the story becomes chaotic, and chaos is the fastest way to make people check out. The story can have twists, but it needs a steady voice guiding it.

Emotions Are Contagious: Whether it's excitement or frustration, your emotions will ripple through your team like a domino effect. If you lose your cool, your employees will either mirror that frustration or withdraw completely. And that withdrawal? It's the death of engagement.

Trust is Fragile: When your emotions spiral, it shakes your employees' trust in you. They begin to wonder if the ship is going to sink. Once that trust is broken, it's hard to rebuild. Employees aren't just leaving the company; they're leaving a story they no longer believe in.

How Emotional Control Helps You Tell a Better Story

Imagine a storyteller who can't control their emotions—a horror novel author who starts crying in the middle of a suspenseful scene or a motivational speaker who breaks down into rage. The story unravels, and so does the audience's interest. Similarly, if you can't manage your emotions in business, you can't expect your employees to remain invested in the long-term narrative of your company.

Here's how Emotional Control, as a storytelling element, helps:

Keeps the Story Focused: By staying composed, you keep the story moving in the right direction. No one likes a story that gets derailed by a temper tantrum.

Creates Stability: Employees crave stability, especially when things go sideways. If you can keep your cool, they'll stick around, believing in the company's ability to handle challenges. Your emotional control becomes the anchor they hold onto.

Builds Empathy: A storyteller who controls their emotions can still express vulnerability without falling apart. That balance builds empathy with the audience—in your case, your employees. When you show that you can manage difficult situations without losing your head, your team feels safe and respected.

Bringing Emotional Control into Your Leadership Story

So, how do you weave Emotional Control into your leadership narrative? Start by recognizing that every situation is part of the broader story you're telling about your company. When things go wrong—and trust me, they will—it's an opportunity to demonstrate resilience and focus. Here's how:

Pause Before Reacting: In storytelling, timing is everything.

Why Your Employees Walk Away When You Lose Your Cool

Before reacting to a problem, take a moment to gather your thoughts. Even a few seconds can mean the difference between snapping and leading with clarity.

Acknowledge Your Emotions, Don't Deny Them: Emotional control doesn't mean you suppress your feelings. It means you recognize them and respond constructively. A great storyteller uses emotions as tools, not weapons.

Create Emotional Safety for Your Team: By managing your own emotions, you allow your employees to feel safe expressing theirs. If they know their leader won't explode under pressure, they'll be more likely to open up about problems before they become crises.

Remember the Bigger Picture: In moments of frustration, it's easy to lose sight of the broader story. Always remind yourself—and your team—of the long-term vision. Keep the story alive, even when the chapter feels bleak.

That Monday morning, when I lost my cool, was a turning point for me. I realized that leadership isn't just about driving results—it's about guiding people through the ups and downs of the journey without ever losing sight of the destination. My story, their story, our story—it all depends on how I choose to tell it, even in the hard times.

In the years that followed, I learned to temper my frustrations and keep the narrative intact. Emotional control became not just a leadership skill, but a storytelling technique that helped me build a team that felt safe, engaged, and connected to the bigger picture. And when my employees started seeing the vision through my calm eyes, they stopped walking away.

Ten

Relatability: The Secret Weapon of Every Great Leader

Year 10 - The Decade Milestone

Standing on the stage at our company's decade anniversary event, I couldn't help but feel a rush of memories from the past ten years. Ten years of hustle, dreams, late nights, and high-pressure decisions had led to this very moment. As I looked out at the sea of faces—employees, investors, partners—I realized something had shifted. The people sitting in front of me weren't just employees; they were believers in the vision I had once struggled to communicate.

It wasn't always like this. In fact, if someone had told me five years ago that I'd be here celebrating not just a company's success, but the emotional investment of everyone in the room, I would've laughed. Back then, I was the "vision guy." The leader who thought sheer passion could inspire others, even if they didn't fully grasp what I was talking about. But as the years went by, I learned a truth that now felt like second nature: Relatability is the secret weapon of every great leader.

The Turning Point: Year 10 and Our Decade Celebration

Our decade anniversary wasn't just a celebration of hitting a milestone—it was an opportunity to see the results of relatability in action. I remember feeling like the company had finally hit its stride because my team wasn't just working for a paycheck or chasing a title anymore. They were living the story, just as I was.

As I stood in front of them, I thought back to the fifth key element of storytelling that had transformed the way I led: relatability.

Step 5: Relatability – Building a Bridge, Not a Pedestal

Five years ago, I had a major realization. No matter how visionary I was or how clear my goals, I couldn't connect with my team unless they could see themselves in the story. If my team saw me as some untouchable figure—the "genius entrepreneur" up on a pedestal—how could they ever feel like they were a part of this journey? They had to see themselves in the vision.

Relatability wasn't about watering down the vision. It was about making the vision theirs. It was about allowing them to see that the obstacles I faced, the mistakes I made, and the triumphs I achieved were things they could relate to in their own lives.

Why Relatability Is So Crucial in Storytelling

Relatability does something that no other storytelling element can: it builds trust. When people can see themselves in your story, they start to believe that they can contribute to the narrative. It stops being your vision and becomes our vision.

Here's what I discovered about making a story relatable:

Vulnerability Connects: People relate to flaws, not perfection. I began sharing my missteps as openly as my successes. At first, it felt like I was exposing weaknesses, but what I was really doing was humanizing myself. When I told my employees about the time I almost quit in Year 3 because we were on the brink of bankruptcy, I saw them nodding—not because they pitied me, but because they'd been there too. They had felt the pressure of failure in their own roles.

Shared Experience Strengthens Loyalty: Relatability turns abstract goals into concrete, shared experiences. I started drawing on experiences they could connect with. Instead of saying, "We're going to be the best company in the market," I began framing it like, "Remember how tough that project was last year? That was us pushing past the impossible. Imagine if we did that for every client, every project. We've done it before, and we can do it again." This shifted the narrative from a distant goal to something they had already experienced with me.

My Story

The Power of 'We': Relatability is the art of transforming "I" into "we." Over time, my language changed. I stopped talking about my story and started talking about our story. Employees aren't drawn to a CEO who talks about their greatness; they're drawn to a leader who helps them see how they're part of that greatness. Once I made that shift, I wasn't just inspiring them—they were inspiring each other.

Relatability in Action: The Decade Event

At our decade event, I didn't just get up on stage and talk about how far the company had come. I told the story of how we got here together. I shared a few stories from the early years—times when we almost didn't make payroll, or when a client disaster nearly sunk a deal—but I didn't position myself as the hero. I pointed out key moments where individuals in the room stepped up, took ownership, and saved the day.

I told the story of Sarah, one of our project managers, who took on a monumental client project when I was about to lose hope. She turned it around when I couldn't see the light at the end of the tunnel. Or Raj, who restructured an entire division during a crisis when the rest of us were too deep in panic mode to think straight. These weren't just success stories—they were moments of shared humanity.

And then something remarkable happened. My employees started telling their stories. As we celebrated, they shared their own versions of those events, how they felt, how they almost quit but didn't, and how they came to believe in the vision themselves. It was a storytelling domino effect.

Relatability: The Secret Weapon of Every Great Leader

How Relatability Builds Their Story

At that moment, I realized relatability didn't just build my story—it built their story. When employees see themselves in the story, they become more invested in the outcome. They don't feel like they're just working for a paycheck; they feel like they're part of something bigger, something personal.

By making my struggles, successes, and vision relatable, I was no longer the only one pushing this dream forward. I had an army of believers behind me. This event marked the culmination of ten years of hard lessons, but it also revealed the power of a simple truth: when people can see themselves in your story, they stop being employees—they become partners in your journey.

Takeaway for the Reader: How to Build Your Own Relatable Story

If you want to build a story that people connect with, here's what you need to do:

Share Your Struggles: Don't be afraid to show vulnerability. The more human you are, the more relatable you become.

Make It About 'Us': Shift your language from "I" to "we." Your employees are not side characters; they're the co-authors of your company's narrative.

Celebrate Their Contributions: Highlight the moments where your team made the impossible happen. This reinforces the idea that the vision doesn't exist without them.

My Story

Relatability isn't just about telling your story—it's about making your team feel like it's their story too. When you can do that, you'll have a group of employees who are more than just workers; they'll become your most passionate advocates.

And that's the real secret weapon of every great leader.

III

The Cost of a Weak Narrative

Attrition and Employee Disengagement

Eleven

The Silent Exodus: How Misalignment Leads to Attrition

Year Eleven: A New Start, or So I Thought

Year Eleven wasn't supposed to feel like Year One, but it did. Not in the exciting, fresh-faced, starry-eyed way, though. This wasn't the thrill of diving into something new with boundless optimism. It was more like watching everything I had built over the last decade quietly unravel, one thread at a time. It was the year I realized that something wasn't quite right beneath the surface. The company, which had once felt like an extension of me, started to feel foreign.

I'd spent the first ten years thinking that if I just painted the big picture, my team would fill in the details. But somewhere along the line, I missed the mark. And they missed it with me.

My Story

It was the year of the silent exodus.

The Quiet Departure of Alignment

It didn't happen all at once. Employees didn't storm out, hurling resignation letters in my face or shaking their fists at the sky. No, it was more subtle, like sand slipping through my fingers. People I thought were in for the long haul—the ones who had been there since the early days—started to leave. Not just physically, but mentally.

I'd walk into meetings, and there'd be this invisible wall between me and my team. They'd nod along, but their eyes…they didn't light up like they used to. I didn't understand it at first. These were the same people who had celebrated every milestone with me, fought through every challenge by my side. But now, they seemed like passengers on a train, waiting for their stop, detached from the destination.

That's when it hit me. We were no longer aligned. The vision I had been clinging to so tightly, the one that had driven every decision, wasn't their vision anymore. And I hadn't noticed.

Stepping Back to Move Forward

It was humbling, realizing that I was no longer the central character in this story. My ego wanted to take control, to fix things, to micromanage and get everything back on track. But there was a whisper in the back of my mind, telling me that the answer wasn't in trying harder—it was in stepping back.

The Silent Exodus: How Misalignment Leads to Attrition

I started letting go. Slowly at first. I gave my employees more room to make decisions, to take ownership, to lead. What surprised me the most wasn't that they stepped up—it was that they had always been ready to step up. I had just been too focused on steering the ship to notice.

The Year Employees Took Charge

By mid-year, I wasn't just giving them the reins; I was stepping aside completely. And let me tell you, it was terrifying. I had spent over a decade pouring my soul into this company, and now I was handing over the keys to people who hadn't been there from Day One. But something incredible happened.

Instead of faltering, the company thrived. The employees took charge in ways I never imagined. They brought new ideas to the table, explored opportunities I hadn't even considered, and handled challenges without running everything by me. I realized that in the years I had been trying to drive the company, I had actually been holding it back from its full potential.

It wasn't that my leadership wasn't needed—it's just that it was no longer needed in the same way. They didn't need me to be the one with all the answers; they needed me to trust them to find the answers themselves.

Growth in My Absence

As my employees started to run the show, I did something I hadn't allowed myself to do in years: I stepped away. And not just for a long weekend. I stepped away for real.

My Story

At first, it was uncomfortable. I'd wake up in the morning, wondering what fire needed to be put out, which project required my oversight. But the phone didn't ring. The emails didn't flood in. The only thing that came in was the company's quarterly report—a report that showed growth beyond anything I had projected.

I took this newfound freedom to pursue the things I had always wanted to do but had been too entrenched in the daily grind to explore. I started investing in passion projects, diving into personal hobbies, and exploring business opportunities outside my core company. And the best part? The company kept growing without me.

In fact, the investments I made while the team was steering the ship doubled. I wasn't just seeing financial returns; I was witnessing the personal growth of the people who had once only followed my lead. Now, they were leading on their own.

A Company That Thrives Without You

That's the moment I realized something profound: I had built a company that could not only survive but thrive without me at the helm. And it wasn't because I had done everything right. It was because I had finally done the one thing I had resisted for too long: I had allowed others to take ownership of the vision. It was no longer just my story—it was our story.

As the year closed, I looked back at Year Eleven not as a failure, but as the turning point where I stopped being a bottleneck and started being the architect of a self-sustaining enterprise.

The Silent Exodus: How Misalignment Leads to Attrition

My employees didn't just carry the company forward—they evolved it. And in doing so, they allowed me to rediscover my passion, knowing that what I had built would outlast my direct involvement.

Year Eleven may have felt like Year One all over again, but this time, it wasn't about starting from scratch. It was about starting fresh, with the knowledge that a vision is only as strong as the people who believe in it. And sometimes, those people need the space to take charge of the story themselves.

Reflection: What I Learned from Letting Go

Looking back, the silent exodus wasn't the departure of employees. It was the departure of my need to control everything. The real misalignment wasn't between me and the team—it was between me and the evolving needs of the business. By stepping aside, I gave my employees the chance to step up, and in return, the company grew beyond anything I could have imagined.

Year Eleven was about trust. Trusting my team to take the story forward, trusting myself to step back, and realizing that the next chapter wasn't mine to write alone.

Twelve

The Mirror Effect: Seeing Your Company Through Your Employees' Eyes

Year twelve: The Year That Felt Like Starting Over

I remember the twelfth year in my entrepreneurial journey vividly, not because it was smooth sailing, but because it felt like a second start. Ironically, it mirrored year two in so many ways. The excitement of building something new, the uncertainty of whether it would work, the anxiety of stepping back into a role that felt unfamiliar—it all came rushing back. But this time, there was one huge difference: I wasn't the one taking the lead. My employees were.

In year two, it was all me. I had the vision, the drive, and the energy to put in 80-hour weeks to make things happen. I was the first in and the last out, watching every detail of the business with the obsessive eyes of a parent. But here I was, in year eleven, feeling the same tension but without the urge to control everything. The mirror had turned, and for the first time, I saw my company not through my eyes but through theirs—my employees.

The Employee Revolution: They Took Charge, I Let Go

By year twelfth, I had done what many founders fear most—I had let go. Not because I wanted to, but because I had no choice. Burnout had whispered in my ear the previous year, and I knew it wasn't just about me anymore. The team was bigger, stronger, more capable. It was time for them to take charge, and as much as I hesitated, I had to trust them to steer the ship.

It wasn't an overnight decision. It was a gradual process where I allowed myself to delegate more and watch from the sidelines, not with nervousness, but with cautious optimism. The surprising thing? My employees didn't just take the reins— they thrived with them. It was as if the collective knowledge, passion, and understanding of the company had finally found its way into their hands.

The business grew that year in ways I couldn't have anticipated. Decisions that used to require my signature now moved forward without hesitation. Problems that would have stressed me out were being solved by a team that had grown confident and competent. They weren't just "my employees" anymore. They were the stewards of the vision, the ones who were living the dream I had built—almost like it was their own.

My Story

Seeing the Company Through Their Eyes

What struck me most was how they saw the company differently from me. To me, this company was my creation, something I'd poured my life into. But to them, it was their opportunity. It was a platform where they could exercise their own creativity, leadership, and ambition.

The little things I had once obsessed over didn't matter to them. They focused on the big picture, on growth, on scaling what I had built. They saw the company not as a reflection of me but as a reflection of them. And that's when it clicked—if I wanted this business to thrive, it couldn't just be "my" company anymore. It had to be theirs. They had to feel ownership over it, not just because they were employees, but because they were the ones making the decisions that defined its future.

This was the mirror effect in its purest form. For the first time, I saw what they saw: potential, untapped markets, new products, and fresh ideas. I realized that my vision, which had fueled the company for so long, was no longer enough. It had to evolve with the people who were now driving it. And in turn, they saw what I saw in them: leaders, creators, and visionaries in their own right.

Stepping Aside to Do What I Love

In many ways, year eleven was liberating. I finally had the space to step aside and do what I truly loved—mentoring, innovating, and thinking about the future without the pressure of daily operations. It was a strange sensation, almost like becoming an advisor to my own company rather than its heart and soul. But it felt right.

I spent that year focusing on the parts of the business that had always intrigued me but that I had never had time to explore. I got back to reading, writing, and engaging in strategic partnerships that I had put on the back burner for too long. For the first time in nearly a decade, I wasn't a bottleneck. The company kept growing, evolving, and even thriving in my absence.

The Unexpected Growth in My Absence

The funny thing about letting go is that, sometimes, things work even better without you. By stepping back, I gave my team the autonomy to make decisions they wouldn't have felt empowered to make with me in the room. They were bolder, more innovative, and less afraid to take risks. The result? Our revenue doubled that year, our investments paid off in ways I couldn't have predicted, and the company started expanding into markets I hadn't even considered.

My absence wasn't a loss for the company—it was an opportunity for them to grow. And grow they did. It was the year we launched three new products, broke into two new international markets, and secured partnerships that catapulted us into a new tier of competition.

Reflecting on the Mirror

Year twelfth was transformative, not because of what I did, but because of what they did. When I looked into the mirror, I saw a company that had outgrown me in the best possible way. I had planted the seed, but now the forest was flourishing on its own. And that's when I realized—the real power of a company isn't in its founder but in the people who carry the vision forward.

This was no longer just my story. It was our story, told through the eyes of every employee who had taken the reins and made the company their own. In many ways, year eleven wasn't the end of the road—it was the beginning of something entirely new. A company where everyone, from the newest hire to the senior executives, had a hand in shaping the future. And that future was looking brighter than ever.

Year twelfth Reflection:

Sometimes, stepping aside is the hardest part of leadership, but it's also the most crucial. When your employees see themselves in the vision, they're not just working for you—they're building something they believe in. The mirror effect is powerful: when you see your company through their eyes, you realize that success doesn't come from control—it comes from trust.

Thirteen

When Passion Isn't Enough: What's Missing from Your Vision

It's hard to believe that after thirteen years as an entrepreneur, I would find myself back at the starting line. Not the same line as when I first began, full of excitement and naive ambition, but a new starting point—one that didn't revolve around me as much as I had once thought it should. Ironically, this thirteenth year felt more like the third, a time when the flame of passion still burned brightly, but the reality had already settled in. Only this time, it wasn't just about me anymore.

In the third year, I thought passion was the secret ingredient. I believed if I poured enough of it into my work, others would pick it up, drink it in, and fuel themselves with it. I was wrong. Passion may ignite a flame, but without something deeper, something more personal to the ones you want to lead, it doesn't last. Here I was again, a decade later, realizing that passion wasn't enough to carry my vision forward. It wasn't about my fire—it was about their light.

This was the year I handed over the reins.

Up until now, my employees had been there for support. They were the doers, the executors, and the fuel for my vision. But this year was different. This was the year they stopped following my lead and started creating their own paths within the company. It was unsettling at first. Watching as they took my ideas—my carefully constructed framework—and began to reshape it with their own hands. They tore down walls I thought were essential, abandoned processes I believed were non-negotiable. At first, I saw it as a threat. But I quickly realized, this was exactly what needed to happen for growth.

You see, I had spent twelve years making the company about me. It was my dream, my passion, my vision. But here in the thirteenth year, I learned that true growth doesn't happen when you force your vision on others. It happens when you detach enough to let others take ownership of it. Detachment became the ultimate form of attachment. As much as I loved this company, I realized I couldn't hold onto it like it was a precious artifact. It had to be a living, breathing organism, capable of evolving on its own. The more I detached, the more it grew, not because I wasn't involved, but because I stopped controlling every single move.

In many ways, I became a spectator, watching as my employees, my partners, and the entrepreneurs around me built on the foundation I had laid. I wasn't stepping away—I was stepping

When Passion Isn't Enough: What's Missing from Your Vision

back. They didn't need my constant oversight; they needed my support. My vision had grown into something far larger than I could have imagined, but it needed more than one person to sustain it.

This is the year I learned what it truly meant to be a leader of leaders, rather than just a leader of employees. My role shifted drastically. I became less of the hands-on entrepreneur I had been for over a decade, and more of a mentor, a guide for the emerging entrepreneurs around me. I wasn't just building a company anymore; I was building other visionaries. I trained over a hundred entrepreneurs this year alone, each of them taking their first steps into building something meaningful. Their visions needed nurturing, their ideas needed support, and it wasn't about my success anymore. It was about theirs.

I discovered that passion could only take me so far, and the same went for them. What they needed—and what I had missed—was the support system to transform that passion into something sustainable. Systems, processes, accountability, and a community that believed in their vision as much as they did. They didn't need me to stand over their shoulders, dictating every move. They needed me to empower them, to teach them how to take the reins and lead their own teams, their own companies.

Looking back, it's almost humorous. In year three, I thought the future of the company relied solely on me. In year thirteen, I realized the future was about letting go, allowing others to step up and fuel the growth that I had once tried to manage alone. What I thought mattered—my passion, my drive—was important, yes, but it wasn't enough. It was never enough. What truly mattered was giving others the opportunity to grow their own passion, to make decisions, to change the status quo, and to take the company to heights I couldn't reach on my own.

Year thirteen taught me that detachment doesn't mean disinterest. It means trust. It means having faith in the people around you to carry the torch, knowing that they'll light up new paths you couldn't see. It was no longer about being the one at the front of the charge, but about standing alongside them, sometimes behind them, and watching as their visions took shape.

I wasn't just leading employees anymore—I was mentoring the next generation of entrepreneurs. And in doing so, I became something more than just the visionary of a company. I became the visionary behind a hundred new dreams, each one fueling the future in ways I hadn't even begun to imagine.

This was the year I became a teacher, a trainer, a builder of entrepreneurs. And in letting go of my vision, I found that it had grown far beyond what I could ever have built alone.

In this chapter, the personal journey of year thirteen is about stepping back and watching as others grow, build, and evolve the original vision, all while learning that true leadership often means empowering others to take control.

Fourteen

Vision Fatigue: Why Your Team is Checked Out

Fourteen years in, and the faces that once lit up at the mention of a new idea now seemed distant, eyes glazed over as I spoke. It felt eerily familiar, like a trip back to Year Four—the first time I fought for control over a vision my team couldn't quite grasp. But this time, the roles were reversed. Instead of me battling to lead, it was my colleagues, the same ones who once pushed back against my ideas, who now needed me to guide them out of their own misguided actions.

Year Four: The Fight for Control

In the fourth year of building my company, I remember feeling like I was constantly wrestling for control. Every meeting turned into a showdown. I'd lay out my vision for the future—what we could be, how we could revolutionize the market—but my colleagues would push back. They weren't wrong, but they weren't right either. They saw the cracks in my plan, pointing out the logistical flaws, the financial risks, and the fact that I was too emotionally tied to the dream.

Back then, I fought to keep my vision alive. To me, it was everything. But my colleagues weren't buying in because they couldn't see themselves in the picture I was painting. They were logical, rational, and wary of the ambition I was pushing. I didn't realize it then, but their reluctance was the first sign of vision fatigue. My team was mentally exhausted, struggling to keep up with a dream that seemed ever-changing, abstract, and distant.

And as I pressed harder, I alienated them. Instead of collaborating, I fought to control. Instead of inspiring, I demanded. It wasn't until things started to crack—small mistakes, missed deadlines, awkward silences in meetings—that I realized my team had checked out.

I had assumed their disengagement was because they didn't believe in my vision. But looking back, it was because they had lost their connection to it. They were tired of fighting for a dream that didn't feel like theirs anymore. That year, I learned that vision wasn't just about leadership; it was about shared ownership.

Year Fourteen: The Fight Revisited

Fast forward ten years, and here I was again—but this time, it wasn't my fight. It was theirs. The very colleagues who had

Vision Fatigue: Why Your Team is Checked Out

once questioned my vision were now clinging to their own rigid ideas. They had become what I once was: leaders too emotionally attached to a plan that no one else could see or support.

They were making decisions that I knew, from experience, would lead us into trouble. They were pushing forward with blinders on, convinced that their way was the only way, just like I had done in Year Four. The irony wasn't lost on me. Back then, I had been the stubborn visionary; now I was the mentor watching them walk down the same misguided path.

At first, I wanted to let them learn the hard way. After all, they had once fought me when I tried to push through my ideas. But leadership isn't about revenge or vindication; it's about growth and guidance. So I stepped in—not as the visionary trying to take control, but as the mentor who had been down that road before.

Vision Fatigue: The Warning Signs

What I had failed to recognize back in Year Four, and what my colleagues were missing now in Year Fourteen, was the creeping sense of vision fatigue. It happens to every team eventually. You work so hard for so long that the dream starts to lose its shine. The future seems less like a thrilling unknown and more like an exhausting uphill battle.

Vision fatigue sets in when your team starts to feel like passengers instead of co-pilots. When they feel like they're just executing tasks without understanding—or believing in—

where those tasks are leading. This was what I saw happening now. The team wasn't rebelling because they didn't care; they were checked out because they were tired of being led in circles. They didn't feel connected to the bigger picture anymore.

But unlike Year Four, I now had the wisdom to recognize the signs early:

Lack of Enthusiasm: The spark that had once lit up our brainstorming sessions was gone. People showed up, but they weren't present.

Surface-Level Engagement: My team was completing their tasks, but there was no depth, no passion. They were doing what they had to, but their hearts weren't in it.

Frustration Brewing: Meetings felt more like tense negotiations than collaborative discussions. People were quick to point out problems, but slow to offer solutions.

Confusion About the Future: The team seemed more confused than excited about where we were heading. There was no shared understanding of the destination.

The Mentor Role: Correcting the Course

As much as I wanted to shout, "I told you so," I knew better now. Instead, I took on the role my team needed: mentor. I sat down with my colleagues, just like they had done with me a decade earlier, and explained why their approach wasn't working. But instead of fighting for control, I asked questions.

"Do you remember when you told me I was too close to my own vision to see the flaws? Well, now it's your turn. What are we missing?"

At first, there was resistance. After all, no one likes to hear that their plan isn't working. But slowly, the walls came down. We started talking openly about the cracks we were all seeing. I didn't come in as the visionary telling them they were wrong; I came in as the mentor helping them see the bigger picture.

Together, we recalibrated. We reminded ourselves of the company's core purpose, the shared dream that had brought us all together in the first place. I made sure they understood that this wasn't about me reclaiming control, but about us rediscovering our shared vision. The vision needed to evolve, but it couldn't be owned by one person—it had to be a collective journey again.

Reflection: The Circle of Leadership

Looking back, Year Four was about me learning to let go of control and invite others into the vision. Year Fourteen was about teaching my colleagues the same lesson. Vision fatigue is real, but it's not the end of the road—it's a sign that the vision needs to be shared, reignited, and reconnected to the hearts of the people who are helping build it.

This time, I knew that fighting for control wasn't the answer. Leadership isn't about holding onto the reins so tightly that you lose your team along the way. It's about guiding, supporting, and sometimes stepping back to let others learn and grow.

The vision will always evolve. But as long as the team feels

My Story

like they're part of the story, they won't check out. They'll stay, fight, and build it with you.

And that's the lesson of Year Fourteen—mentorship, not control, is the key to keeping the dream alive.

Fifteen

Why Good Employees Don't Stick Around for Bad Stories

Year Fifteen of My Entrepreneurial Journey

Year fifteen wasn't just another milestone for me; it was a mirror. I had learned a lot about vision, storytelling, and leadership by this point, but that year taught me one of the most profound lessons of my career—sometimes, the best way to strengthen your own narrative is to watch others fumble with theirs.

I had reached a point where I thought I had finally nailed down my vision. The company was growing, our reputation was solid, and new hires were lining up to join us. But there was a growing sense of unease that I couldn't quite put my finger on. Employees I valued—brilliant, innovative people—were quietly leaving. It wasn't an exodus, not yet, but it felt like the start of something unsettling.

My Story

Meanwhile, my peers—other entrepreneurs and leaders I had mentored over the years—seemed to be going through the same thing. Except for them, it was worse. They had one thing in common: a talent for crafting bad stories.

Now, by "bad stories," I don't mean they didn't know how to sell their vision. Oh, no. They could deliver a rousing speech, host a strategy session, and draw up the most colorful PowerPoint you've ever seen. But something was always off. Their stories lacked heart. They were full of facts and figures but completely devoid of connection.

I watched them fumble with this—one by one. These were people with fantastic ideas, bold visions, and promising futures, but they struggled to get their teams on board. They couldn't keep their employees. And while they blamed competition, salary, or "generational differences," I knew better. Their employees weren't leaving for greener pastures; they were running from stories they couldn't connect with.

The Art of Fumbling

It became clear to me that year that good employees—those who care, who innovate, who take ownership—don't stick around for bad stories. I watched as one of my colleagues tried to launch a new product line, but his employees were half-hearted at best. His story lacked personal stakes. His team saw it as just another task to complete. They couldn't see how they fit into the bigger picture, and when things got tough, they started bailing.

I could see their body language in meetings—eyes glazed

Why Good Employees Don't Stick Around for Bad Stories

over, hands fiddling with phones. They were present, but not engaged. It was like they were there but already gone, disconnected from the journey they were supposed to be on.

On the flip side, I noticed something happening in my own company. I had started to correct my narrative over the past few years, slowly weaving in more personal moments, more vulnerability. I didn't just talk about our goals; I talked about why those goals mattered to me—and why they should matter to the team. I realized that my story had shifted from being about me to being about us. And that was the turning point.

Learning from Their Mistakes

Here's where it gets interesting: the lessons I learned that year didn't come from my own efforts, but from watching others flounder. I saw all the things they were doing wrong, and it forced me to reflect on what I had been doing right—sometimes unintentionally.

The entrepreneurs around me would sell a vision, but they didn't invite their employees to become part of the story. They treated their teams like audience members instead of co-authors. And you could feel it in the air. People were walking out, not because they didn't believe in the company, but because they couldn't see themselves in the future that was being painted.

One of my colleagues—let's call him Dave—was the most vivid example. Dave had a booming tech startup. Fast-growing, well-funded, the works. But turnover was through the roof. I'll never forget sitting down with him over coffee that year. His frustration was palpable.

"I don't get it," he said. "I'm offering them stock options, high salaries, perks—everything they could want. But they keep leaving. What am I doing wrong?"

I didn't have the heart to tell him then, but I knew exactly what he was doing wrong. His story was missing them. It was just a monologue, a corporate narrative, void of the emotional substance that binds a team together. And when that happens, even your best people—the ones who want to give their all—start looking elsewhere.

Strengthening My Own Story

Ironically, watching Dave and others like him fumble with their stories helped me refine my own. I realized that the more personal I made my narrative, the more it resonated with my employees. When I spoke about challenges from my perspective but tied them to our collective future, my team leaned in. They weren't just doing a job; they were part of a journey—a journey that felt as much theirs as it did mine.

By year fifteen, my story had evolved. It wasn't just about numbers, products, or market share. It was about the shared experiences we'd had, the failures we'd overcome, and the future we were building together. My employees didn't just listen to my story—they lived it. They saw themselves in it, and that made all the difference.

That year, as I watched colleagues lose their best talent, I held onto mine. Not because I had better perks or bigger paychecks, but because my story was their story too. They didn't stick around for the benefits; they stayed because they believed in the journey we were on together.

The Lesson

Year fifteen taught me this: Good employees don't leave for better opportunities—they leave for better stories. The leaders who can't craft a compelling narrative, one that invites everyone in, will always watch their best people walk away.

The question isn't whether your employees understand the vision; it's whether they see themselves in it.

IV

Crafting a Relatable Vision

Making Your Story Resonate

Sixteen

Your Story Matters: How to Make It Matter to Others

As I stepped into my sixteenth year as an entrepreneur, a realization dawned on me: my story had become more than just my own. It was a collection of experiences, lessons, failures, and victories that resonated not only within my mind but also in the hearts of others. It was time to not only refine my narrative but to share the key elements of storytelling with fellow entrepreneurs. The desire to teach became a driving force, propelling me into a new phase of my journey.

The Transformative Power of Storytelling

I began to understand that storytelling is not just an art; it is a vital skill for any entrepreneur aiming to engage and inspire their audience. It weaves together a narrative that fosters connection, builds trust, and, ultimately, drives action. My experiences over the years became the foundation for a comprehensive approach to storytelling, and I felt compelled to pass this knowledge on.

Key Elements of Effective Storytelling

To help fellow entrepreneurs improve their narratives, I identified several key elements essential for crafting a compelling story. Here's what I taught them:

Authenticity:
How to Use It: Share your genuine experiences, including struggles and triumphs. Authenticity creates trust and allows your audience to relate to you.
Example: Instead of only highlighting your successes, recount the moments of failure that shaped your journey. People connect with vulnerability.

Character:
How to Use It: Position yourself or your customers as the main character. Flesh them out with traits, desires, and struggles to evoke empathy.
Example: Illustrate your journey by describing a particular challenge you faced and how it affected your growth, allowing your audience to see themselves in your story.

Conflict:
How to Use It: Present a challenge or obstacle that must be overcome. This creates tension and keeps your audience engaged.
Example: Share a pivotal moment in your business where everything seemed to go wrong and how you navigated through it, turning the conflict into a lesson.

Resolution:

How to Use It: Conclude your story with a resolution that offers insight or a lesson learned. This helps your audience understand the value of the journey.

Example: After detailing a significant challenge, explain how you resolved it, what you learned, and how that knowledge can be applied in their own lives.

Emotion:

How to Use It: Evoke emotions through your narrative. Use descriptive language and personal anecdotes that resonate on a human level.

Example: When discussing a breakthrough moment, describe the emotions you felt—excitement, fear, joy—to help your audience feel the weight of your journey.

Imagery:

How to Use It: Paint vivid pictures with your words. Help your audience visualize the scenes you describe.

Example: Instead of stating facts, describe the setting, emotions, and reactions that bring your story to life. This makes the experience more relatable.

Call to Action:

How to Use It: Encourage your audience to take action based on the insights shared in your story. This could be a mindset shift or a practical step forward.

Example: After sharing a powerful lesson, challenge your audience to reflect on their own journeys and consider how they can implement changes in their approach.

My Story

Spreading the Message

As I taught these elements to other entrepreneurs, I saw the transformation in their narratives. Each session felt like a collaborative workshop where we dissected stories and rebuilt them into powerful narratives. We practiced storytelling exercises, exchanged feedback, and shared our own journeys. I was amazed at how some simple adjustments in their approach turned mundane pitches into gripping tales.

Real-Life Impact

One particular entrepreneur, Lisa, shared her story of overcoming adversity in her startup journey. By integrating the key elements, she transformed her pitch from a list of accomplishments into a heartfelt narrative that captivated investors. The result? She secured funding and built a loyal customer base, all thanks to a story that resonated deeply.

Reflections

In this sixteenth year, I learned that storytelling is not just about crafting an engaging narrative; it's about creating a connection that leads to shared understanding and growth. By teaching others the essential elements of storytelling, I not only enriched their narratives but also strengthened the fabric of our entrepreneurial community.

As I continued to hone my own story, I realized that the impact of sharing this knowledge would extend far beyond individual success; it would foster a culture where stories mattered—where every entrepreneur's journey was valued, understood, and connected to the greater narrative of innovation and resilience.

With this foundation laid, I looked forward to the next chapter, eager to see how the stories we created would ripple through our community, sparking inspiration and igniting change. After all, in the end, our stories mattered—not just for us, but for everyone willing to listen.

Seventeen

The Leadership Vacuum: Filling It with a Compelling Narrative

Year 17 – The Year of Crafting and Teaching the Art of Storytelling

By the time I hit my 17th year as an entrepreneur, I realized something profound—success wasn't just about vision or leadership, but about how you communicate that vision. After nearly two decades of building companies, I learned that a compelling narrative could be the difference between leading a team that's merely compliant and one that's truly invested.

The Epiphany: Why Storytelling Is the Missing Ingredient

This was the year I began to understand that in the absence of a strong story, a leadership vacuum formed. People naturally want to follow a story, not just a set of instructions. They want to feel like they're part of something bigger than themselves. A vision without a story is like a ship without wind. It might be going in the right direction, but it's not moving anywhere fast. I had to fill that vacuum.

And not just for myself.

I realized my success depended on helping other entrepreneurs tell their own stories better. So, I spent Year 17 teaching the essential elements of storytelling, the very same tools that transformed my own leadership journey, to others.

The Key Elements of a Compelling Narrative
1. The Hero's Journey

At the heart of every great story is a hero. In the case of entrepreneurship, that hero could be you, the founder, or your company as a whole. But here's the twist: your employees, colleagues, and even customers should also see themselves as part of this journey.

The hero's journey has three key phases:

Departure: The hero (you) embarks on a challenge or pursuit. This could be the founding of the company or the mission you're chasing.

Struggle: Every story needs conflict. Whether it's market challenges, financial setbacks, or internal struggles, these difficulties shape the story.

Resolution: How the hero (or company) overcomes those challenges is where employees connect emotionally. They want to be part of that victory.

Application: I taught fellow entrepreneurs to place their employees into the story as co-heroes, experiencing the struggles, contributing to the resolutions. This way, the company's victories become personal achievements for everyone involved.

2. Emotion Over Facts

People may remember statistics, but they never forget how a story makes them feel. Great storytelling doesn't bombard the audience with numbers or strategic goals; it connects on an emotional level. The key is to tell stories that humanize the business: anecdotes of perseverance, stories of the struggles we overcame as a team, and personal victories within the company.

Application: I showed entrepreneurs how to integrate emotional triggers—joy, fear, frustration, hope—into their narrative. Employees relate to vulnerability and success stories that show real people overcoming real obstacles, which is much more engaging than dry business objectives.

3. Relatability: Making Your Story Their Story

One of the biggest mistakes I see entrepreneurs make is forgetting that their story has to resonate with their audience—employees or colleagues. The more relatable the story, the easier it is for people to feel invested. This means understanding the background, struggles, and motivations of your team members and reflecting those in your narrative.

Application: I encouraged leaders to research their employees' backgrounds. What challenges have they faced? What are their personal goals? Weave those into the company's larger mission. A company striving for greatness is relatable when it's tied to individual aspirations. For example, "Just like you've worked hard to provide for your family, we work hard to grow this company, and together, we'll succeed."

4. Conflict: The Glue of Good Stories

No story is complete without conflict. Too many leaders want to gloss over the hard times, hoping to inspire solely through the vision of a bright future. But without showing the bumps in the road—the mistakes, the failures, the hard lessons—you lose authenticity, and more importantly, the empathy of your audience.

Application: I emphasized the importance of transparency. Leaders must be open about the company's struggles—whether it's financial hurdles or missteps in decision-making. By doing this, employees feel they're navigating the tough waters with you, not being shielded from reality. This also sets the stage for greater celebration when the challenges are overcome.

5. The Call to Action

A story without action is just entertainment. In the business world, a narrative should always lead to a clear call to action for the audience. Whether that's committing to a new initiative or stepping up as a leader within the team, your story must drive your employees toward taking concrete steps.

Application: I trained other entrepreneurs to end their stories not with a conclusion, but with a new beginning—challenging employees to step into their role as heroes. For instance, "We've faced immense challenges together, but this is where the real journey begins. How will you help us write the next chapter?"

Crafting Stories that Resonate with Your Audience

The best narratives don't just come from the storyteller's mind—they are deeply influenced by the listeners themselves. In my 17th year, I worked with countless entrepreneurs to tailor their stories to the backgrounds, struggles, and values of their employees. If you want people to become emotionally invested, they need to see their own reflections in the narrative you're telling.

6. Understanding Your Audience's Struggles

Employees aren't blank slates. They bring their own life experiences, fears, and ambitions to the workplace. The key to a successful pitch is acknowledging that. For example, if you're addressing a team that has been through layoffs, you might highlight the struggles the company faced in order to survive and how the team's resilience was integral to turning things around.

Application: I coached leaders to actively listen to their teams before crafting any story. The more you know about your team's individual challenges, the more personalized your story becomes. This level of personalization helps employees feel understood and valued.

7. Tying Personal and Professional Stories Together

Another vital element I stressed was the blending of personal and professional narratives. Leaders often isolate their professional struggles from their personal stories, but employees are more likely to connect with a holistic narrative—one that shows how the personal journey impacts the professional one.

The Leadership Vacuum: Filling It with a Compelling...

Application: For example, I shared stories of how I balanced personal struggles—family health crises or financial stress—with running a business. This level of honesty and vulnerability encourages employees to relate, seeing leadership as human and understanding that their own personal battles are part of their growth within the company.

Teaching the Art of Storytelling

By the end of Year 17, I had developed not just my own storytelling ability, but I had also begun teaching these principles to other entrepreneurs. I hosted workshops, webinars, and one-on-one coaching sessions to help them identify the gaps in their communication and fill those leadership vacuums with powerful, compelling narratives.

The Power of Collective Narratives

In this year, I fully realized that the most effective stories are those that are co-authored. It's not just about you, the entrepreneur, telling the story—it's about inviting your team to contribute to it. When employees see themselves as part of the story, they become more than passive listeners; they become co-creators, fully invested in the company's success.

Conclusion: Year 17's Lesson Year 17 was a pivotal year—both in refining my own leadership story and in teaching others how to fill their own leadership vacuums. By focusing on emotional resonance, relatability, conflict, and a strong call to action, I learned that stories aren't just a tool for communication—they are the driving force behind loyalty, engagement, and success.

If you want your employees to follow you, don't just give them a vision. Give them a narrative they want to be a part of.

Eighteen

Narrative Identity: Why Your Employees Should See Themselves in Your Vision

The Year I Became a Mentor of Stories

In the eighteenth year of my journey as an entrepreneur, I had begun to see the pivotal role that storytelling played not just in my own leadership but in the development of other entrepreneurs as well. I had spent years crafting my own narrative, learning through trial and error, and now, it was time to share those lessons with others. This was the year I transitioned from simply leading my own team to mentoring other leaders, helping them create narratives that would inspire and involve their employees.

Key Elements of Storytelling: Building a Vision People See Themselves In

My Story

Before diving into the stories I helped shape, let's take a step back and look at the key elements of storytelling that I taught these entrepreneurs. After all, without these elements, any story—no matter how passionate—falls flat. Here's what I helped them understand:

Authenticity:
A story must be real and raw. People don't follow a vision that feels fabricated. Authenticity isn't just about truth; it's about vulnerability. I taught entrepreneurs to peel back the layers of polish and allow their teams to see the human behind the title. I urged them to share both their triumphs and their failures because it's the struggles that make a story relatable.

Relatability:
It's not enough for the entrepreneur's story to be heard; it needs to resonate. I focused on showing leaders how to weave their employees' roles into the fabric of the company's story. The question I asked them to answer was simple but profound: How is this vision relevant to your team's personal and professional growth? When people can see themselves in your story, they naturally become more invested.

Consistency:
A good story isn't told once—it's reiterated, reinforced, and retold in new ways as the journey evolves. I taught leaders to be consistent in their messaging, ensuring that the narrative didn't waver. Their employees needed to hear the same core vision, even if the details changed. This consistency bred trust, and with trust came loyalty.

Emotional Engagement:

Logic may convince, but emotions inspire. I worked on helping entrepreneurs tap into the emotional core of their story. Numbers and data don't spark action, but a heartfelt vision does. We crafted narratives that connected to the core desires of the employees—the desire for purpose, belonging, and impact.

Future-Oriented:

A story rooted only in the past becomes stale. I coached these entrepreneurs to make their narratives forward-looking, where employees could see a future they wanted to be part of. The "what's next" is what keeps people on board, excited for the journey ahead.

Teaching the Art of Storytelling: The Mentorship Begins

That year, I didn't just keep these lessons to myself. I took on several entrepreneurs under my mentorship, guiding them through the process of storytelling as a tool for leadership. Each one of them had a different narrative, but the goal was the same—building a story their teams could see themselves in.

At first, they struggled. Like many leaders, they were accustomed to talking at their employees rather than with them. Some told me, "I don't know if my story matters enough," while others worried, "What if my team doesn't care about this?"

We started by stripping away those doubts. I helped them see that it wasn't about crafting the perfect story; it was about creating one that was real, relatable, and repeatable. As they practiced and evolved their narratives, something incredible happened—their teams started listening, not out of obligation but out of genuine interest.

One entrepreneur, let's call him Arun, had always focused on numbers and goals in his leadership. But once he started telling the story of why those numbers mattered, sharing his personal motivation for success, his team began to buy into the vision with a renewed sense of purpose. Employees saw their roles not just as jobs, but as part of a larger mission. His company's culture transformed in a matter of months.

Evolving Leaders Into Mentors

The most fulfilling part of this year was watching these entrepreneurs evolve—not just as storytellers but as leaders. They began to take their newly learned skills and mentor others within their own companies. It was a ripple effect; as I mentored them, they, in turn, became mentors to their next line of leaders. Their teams grew more engaged, and the cycle of inspiration continued.

By helping them tell their story in a way that made sense to their employees, I wasn't just empowering leaders; I was creating a network of mentorship, where leadership was passed down, not through authority but through shared narrative. Each entrepreneur I mentored became a torchbearer of storytelling, igniting their own teams with the same passion and vision.

The Ones Who Didn't Follow

Of course, not everyone was ready for this transformation. Some entrepreneurs I reached out to weren't willing to embrace storytelling. They were too rooted in their old ways—leading with numbers, managing through hierarchy, and avoiding vulnerability. I wished them well, but without the foundation of narrative identity, they struggled to engage their teams.

Sadly, many of them saw high turnover, disengaged employees, and stagnant growth. I could see the difference between the businesses that embraced storytelling and those that didn't. The companies without a strong narrative couldn't retain their people or their passion. Their teams felt like outsiders, disconnected from the vision and uninspired by the journey.

Looking Back, Looking Forward

By the end of the eighteenth year, I had not only improved my own narrative but had shaped the stories of countless entrepreneurs, turning them into more effective leaders. Those who embraced storytelling as a core leadership skill thrived, with teams who saw themselves as essential parts of the company's mission. They became brand advocates, leaders in their own right, and, ultimately, mentors to others.

Those who didn't? Well, their stories are still waiting to be told—if they ever find the courage to share them.

This chapter marks a turning point in my journey as I shifted from being solely focused on my own leadership to becoming a guide for others. It was here that I fully realized the power of narrative identity, not just in keeping my team engaged but in shaping a new generation of entrepreneurs who could inspire their own followers. This was the year my story became theirs—and theirs, mine.

Nineteen

The Brand Advocate Formula: Turning Skeptics into Believers

Year 19 – The Divide Between Followers and Skeptics

It was the nineteenth year into my entrepreneurial journey, and the cracks in my vision were starting to show—cracks that didn't appear to be structural at first, but more like splinters in the framework of my team. The divide between those who embraced my storytelling-driven approach and those who didn't was becoming glaringly obvious.

I'd been running the business for nearly two decades, weathering countless storms and celebrating victories both big and small. But as I evolved, so did the market, and with that, the need for something more profound than just a vision—a narrative that could drive belief. I had my advocates, those who had become invested in "My Story," and they were flourishing. But on the other side, there were skeptics—team members and colleagues who struggled to keep pace, to believe in the dream, simply because they hadn't bought into the story I was trying to sell.

The Skeptics: Why They Struggled

Some of the people who didn't follow my storytelling strategy were those who believed in the old school of thought. They were firm in their conviction that data, metrics, and bottom-line results were the only things that mattered. They believed stories were fluff—a distraction from the real work. For them, storytelling was just another buzzword in a world obsessed with trends, something they thought would fade away like fidget spinners or kale smoothies.

But here's the thing: they were wrong. And they paid the price for that stubbornness.

Without an emotionally-driven narrative, these skeptics struggled to connect with customers, partners, and even their own teams. Their marketing campaigns were like hollow vessels—technically correct but lacking soul. Their interactions felt transactional, and that made it difficult to build the kind of long-term loyalty that a brand needs to thrive. Sure, they could close deals, but they weren't creating advocates. And in today's world, without advocates, you're just another face in the crowd.

Internally, these skeptics also struggled with employee retention. They couldn't inspire passion in their teams. Why? Because they didn't share their own passion. They believed that showing the numbers, setting goals, and offering compensation were enough. But that's not what drives people. In Year 19, I learned that people want to be part of something bigger. They want to believe in a story they can relate to—a cause that makes them feel connected. My skeptics missed that, and as a result, their teams were disengaged, frequently burned out, and often looking for greener pastures.

One particular senior manager who scoffed at the storytelling approach told me flat out, "I'll get my results with facts, not stories." And for a while, he did get results. But six months later, his department faced record-level turnover, and the projects they were leading started falling apart. Why? Because he was only managing transactions, not relationships. He hadn't turned his employees into advocates for his mission—he was merely guiding them to perform tasks.

The Believers: Why They Thrived

Then there were the others. Those who bought into the idea that storytelling wasn't just for customers, but for everyone involved in the company. These were the ones who took my advice, embraced the power of narrative, and worked with me to craft stories that resonated on every level—internally and externally. They understood that marketing wasn't just about product features but about emotional engagement. They wove storytelling into their daily interactions, team meetings, and marketing strategies.

One of my team leads, let's call her Sarah, stood out. She was a true believer in the art of storytelling. Instead of just presenting quarterly goals to her team, she told them why these goals mattered—not just to the company, but to the individuals working there. She painted a picture of how their success was intertwined with the success of the company's mission. She made them feel like heroes in a larger narrative, and the results spoke for themselves.

Her team not only hit their targets; they went above and beyond. They were excited to come to work because they felt personally connected to the company's story. They weren't just employees—they were brand advocates, passionate about what we were building and proud to represent the company.

Externally, Sarah integrated storytelling into her marketing campaigns. Instead of bombarding potential clients with data and jargon, she focused on customer stories. She shared the success of other clients, turning case studies into narratives where the customers were the protagonists. These stories built trust and emotional connection, which led to longer-lasting relationships and stronger customer loyalty. When we did customer follow-ups, they didn't just see us as a service provider—they saw us as partners who cared about their success.

Marketing Through Stories: Who Thrived and Who Didn't

The brands that embraced storytelling in their integrated marketing campaigns flourished. Those who ignored it, like my skeptics, stagnated. I remember two distinct companies in our industry—one who harnessed the power of storytelling and one who clung to old marketing tactics.

My Story

The first company, let's call them Innovative Solutions, understood that customers don't just buy products—they buy into experiences. They ran campaigns that didn't just explain the features of their services but told the story of why those services mattered. Their campaigns featured customer testimonials, not as cold, hard facts, but as emotional journeys. They focused on the problems their clients faced, how their lives changed because of the product, and the personal impact it had. Their social media posts were filled with authentic, relatable stories of real people, and as a result, their engagement skyrocketed. Customers became advocates, not because they were convinced by data, but because they felt emotionally invested in the story.

On the flip side, there was Traditional Corp, who believed that storytelling was irrelevant in a B2B environment. They stuck to showcasing their product features and threw around industry jargon like confetti. Their marketing campaigns were dry, uninviting, and robotic. Sure, they had a few wins here and there, but their growth stagnated because they couldn't build long-term relationships with their customers. Their clients saw them as a vendor, not a partner, and switched to competitors the moment someone offered a better price or a shinier product.

Turning Skeptics into Believers

In Year 19, the lesson became crystal clear: if you want your team to stay, to believe in what you're doing, and to advocate for your brand, you must tell your story. And not just any story—one that people can see themselves in. The skeptics who didn't get that lesson struggled, constantly fighting fires and dealing with disengaged teams. But those who embraced storytelling

The Brand Advocate Formula: Turning Skeptics into Believers

thrived.

If you want to turn skeptics into believers, both within your company and beyond, the formula is simple: create a narrative that resonates emotionally. Make people feel like they're part of something bigger, and they will become your most loyal advocates.

Twenty

Beyond the Pitch: How to Sell the Future to Your Team

Year Twenty of the Entrepreneurial Journey

In your twentieth year as an entrepreneur, there's an overwhelming feeling of accomplishment. The battle scars are real, but so is the satisfaction of hitting a milestone that many only dream of. But here's the twist—though I stand at the edge of my twentieth year, basking in the victory of survival and growth, my parents have already been here, and they have done so much more.

When I think about this chapter, I can't help but reflect on my dad and mom, who crossed this milestone years ago. They weren't entrepreneurs in the way I am today—no digital revolutions, no flashy pitches, no "team engagement workshops." They worked with their hands, their hearts, and their sheer will. But looking back, I realize they were selling the future every day in their own way. They didn't call it a "pitch," but everything they did was laying the groundwork for something bigger, something lasting.

My father had a way of talking about tomorrow like it was already here. He'd say, "You don't have to convince people to follow you if they believe in the same destination." And that's what I learned from him—selling the future isn't about a perfect presentation; it's about making people see a world that hasn't come to life yet, and somehow making them feel like they're already living in it. That was his magic, his story. And now, as I write this chapter, I realize it's mine too.

This year, as I crossed the twenty-year mark, I began to understand what he meant. The future isn't in the words you say to your team. It's in the way you make them feel connected to something larger than themselves. That's where many entrepreneurs go wrong. They think the pitch is about convincing employees that they're building something great—when in reality, it's about making them feel like they're already part of that greatness.

Building a Future Without Perfect Pitches

In the first ten years of my career, I gave countless presentations, held meetings, and fired up my team with promises of what was to come. I believed in every word I said, but not every person I spoke to could see the future as clearly as I did. And that's the key difference between selling a product and selling the future. A product exists in the present—you can hold it, see it, test it. The future? It's abstract, a vision only visible to those with belief.

For years, I was stuck in this cycle of trying to get my employees to "see" the vision, to feel as excited about it as I did. I would perfect my pitches, try to paint the brightest picture, but there were always a few who just didn't seem to get it. They were like shadows lingering in the background—present, but never truly committed.

And then, it hit me: You don't sell the future with words. You sell it with belief.

I didn't learn this from a book or a podcast, but from watching my mother and father over the years. When they spoke about the future, it wasn't about excitement or big dreams—it was about trust, consistency, and showing up every single day. People followed them because they trusted that wherever they were going, it would be worth it. There was no fanfare, no grand declarations. Just pure belief and hard work.

My Story Isn't Just Mine

As I sit here writing this, it's becoming clear to me that my story isn't just mine. It's theirs. My twenty years of entrepreneurship are built on the back of my parents' understanding of the world and the future. And that's the lesson I want to pass on: The future isn't just about where you're going—it's about who has laid the foundation for you to get there.

In the workplace, that foundation is built by your team's belief in you and their belief in the story you're collectively writing. They have to see themselves as part of something bigger—part of the journey, not just a cog in the wheel.

Selling the Future to Your Team

So, how do you sell the future to your team when you've hit year twenty and they've heard every pitch in the book?

Make Them Co-Authors of the Story

Your employees need to feel like they're writing the future with you. When my parents worked, they made sure everyone involved felt like they were a critical part of the journey. They didn't "lead"; they co-created. It's a powerful mindset shift that transforms a top-down vision into a collective movement.

Show, Don't Just Tell

In the early years, I relied heavily on storytelling through words. But if there's one thing the past decade has taught me, it's that actions speak louder. Show your team the future in small ways every day—through decisions, through transparency, through inclusion.

Create a Culture of Belief

The future is sold not by one person but by an entire culture that believes in it. This is something my parents did instinctively. They created an environment where everyone shared the belief that tomorrow was worth the effort today. If your team doesn't believe in the future you're pitching, no amount of presentations will change that.

Celebrate the Small Wins

Each year of your entrepreneurial journey is like a chapter, and every chapter has its own climax. You don't need to wait for the grand finale to get your team on board. Celebrate the small wins—the steps that show progress toward the bigger picture.

As I reflect on the lessons I've learned from my parents, I realize that I'm not just writing my story; I'm continuing theirs. They taught me that the future is something you live daily, not just something you pitch once in a while. And now, after twenty years, I'm working to ensure that my team feels the same way.

Thank you for taking the time to join me on this journey. If My Story resonates with you or has helped you in any way, I'd love to hear from you. Feel free to leave a testimonial or share your thoughts in the book review section on Amazon. Your support not only helps me but also other readers who may be inspired by the collective stories we are all writing.

Together, we are all selling the future. One chapter at a time.

www.ingramcontent.com/pod-product-compliance
Lightning Source LLC
Chambersburg PA
CBHW070146230526
45471CB00002B/537